FACEBOOK MARKETING SIMPLIFIED

"Unlocking Success: A Simplified Guide to Mastering Facebook Marketing"

VINCENT SIM

Copyright ©

by Vincent Sims 2024 All rights reserved.

Dedication

"To the relentless entrepreneurs navigating the digital realm with ambition and curiosity—may this guide simplify your journey through the intricate landscape of Facebook marketing."

Table of Contents

Acknowledgments

"I extend my heartfelt gratitude to all those who contributed to the creation of this book, 'Facebook Marketing Simplified.' Special thanks to my dedicated team, whose passion and hard work brought this project to life. I am also grateful for the invaluable insights shared by industry experts and the unwavering support from friends and family. Together, we strive to simplify the world of Facebook marketing for every reader."

Preface

Welcome to 'Facebook Marketing Simplified.' In the vast realm of digital strategies, mastering the art of Facebook marketing is pivotal for success. This book is designed as a compass, guiding you through the intricate landscape of social media promotion with clarity and simplicity.

As technology continues to advance, the need for a straightforward approach to Facebook marketing becomes increasingly apparent. This book aims to bridge the gap between complexity and comprehension, offering a distilled guide for individuals and businesses eager to thrive in the dynamic world of online advertising.

Drawing on practical experiences, industry insights, and the ever-changing nature of Facebook algorithms, this guide seeks to equip you with the knowledge needed to navigate this powerful platform effectively. From creating engaging content to optimizing ad campaigns, each chapter is crafted to empower you with actionable steps and strategic understanding.

Whether you're a digital marketing professional, a small business owner, or an aspiring social media enthusiast, 'Facebook Marketing Simplified' is your companion on the journey to harness the full potential of Facebook for your goals.

Embark on this simplified exploration, and let the world of Facebook marketing unfold before you.

[Vincent Sims]

Chapter 1

Introduction to Facebook Marketing

- Overview of the importance of Facebook for marketing

In the dynamic landscape of digital marketing, one platform stands out as a juggernaut for connecting businesses with their audience – Facebook. With over two billion monthly active users globally, Facebook has become an indispensable tool for marketers seeking to establish a robust online presence.

The Importance of Facebook for Marketing

1. Unparalleled Reach:

Facebook's extensive user base provides an unparalleled reach for businesses of all sizes. Whether you are a local enterprise or a global brand, the platform offers the potential to connect with a diverse audience.

2. Targeted Advertising:

One of the defining features of Facebook marketing is its sophisticated targeting capabilities. Marketers can tailor their messages based on demographics, interests, and behaviors, ensuring that content reaches the most relevant audience.

3. Engagement and Interaction:

Facebook is not just a broadcasting platform; it's a dynamic space for engagement. The platform encourages two-way communication, allowing businesses to interact directly with their audience through comments, likes, and shares.

4. Building Brand Loyalty:

Establishing a presence on Facebook provides an opportunity to humanize your brand. Regular and authentic interactions help build trust and loyalty among your audience, fostering a sense of community around your products or services.

5. Insights and Analytics:

Facebook's robust analytics tools empower marketers to track and measure the performance of their campaigns. This data-driven approach allows for continuous optimization, ensuring that marketing efforts align with business goals.

6. Cost-Effective Marketing:
Compared to traditional advertising channels, Facebook offers a cost-effective solution for reaching a large audience. Advertisers can set budgets, control costs, and track return on investment (ROI) with precision.

7. Multimedia Capabilities:
Facebook supports a variety of multimedia formats, including images, videos, and live streaming. This versatility enables marketers to create diverse and engaging content that resonates with their target audience.

In essence, Facebook marketing is not just about creating advertisements; it's about fostering meaningful connections, driving engagement, and ultimately, achieving business objectives. As we delve into the intricacies of Facebook marketing, this guide aims to demystify the process, providing you with the insights and tools needed to leverage this powerful platform effectively. Welcome to the world of Facebook marketing – where possibilities are as vast as your creativity and strategy allow.

- Key benefits and opportunities

1. Audience Targeting Precision:
Facebook's robust advertising platform allows marketers to pinpoint their target audience with exceptional precision. Through demographics, interests, behaviors, and location targeting, businesses can ensure their messages reach the most relevant individuals, optimizing the impact of their campaigns.

2. Enhanced Brand Visibility:
Establishing a presence on Facebook significantly enhances brand visibility. Regularly appearing on users' feeds fosters brand recognition, making it more likely for your business to come to mind when customers are making purchasing decisions.

3. Community Building:

Facebook provides a unique opportunity to create and nurture a community around your brand. Engaging content, discussions, and user-generated content can contribute to a sense of belonging, turning customers into brand advocates.

4. Mobile-First Approach:

Given the prevalence of mobile device usage, Facebook's mobile-friendly platform ensures that marketing content is accessible to users on various devices. This mobile-first approach is crucial in reaching audiences who predominantly engage with content on smartphones and tablets.

5. Insights for Informed Decision-Making:

Facebook's analytics tools offer valuable insights into campaign performance. Marketers can track metrics such as reach, engagement, and conversion rates, enabling data-driven decision-making and continuous optimization for better results.

6. Diverse Content Formats:

The platform supports a variety of content formats, including images, videos, carousels, and stories. This diversity allows marketers to experiment with different types of content to keep their audience engaged and interested.

7. Cost-Effective Advertising:

Facebook's advertising options cater to various budgets. Whether you're a small business or a multinational corporation, the platform's flexible advertising solutions allow for cost-effective campaigns with measurable returns.

8. E-Commerce Integration:

With features like Facebook Shops, businesses can seamlessly integrate e-commerce into their Facebook presence. This integration facilitates a streamlined shopping experience for users, creating a direct path from discovery to purchase.

9. Global Market Reach:

Facebook's global user base provides businesses with an opportunity to reach audiences worldwide. Whether expanding into new markets or connecting with a diverse customer base, the platform offers unparalleled access to a vast and varied audience.

10. Real-Time Interaction:

The real-time nature of Facebook enables businesses to interact with their audience instantly. Timely responses to comments, messages, and feedback contribute to a positive brand image and foster customer satisfaction.

In navigating the landscape of Facebook marketing, recognizing and leveraging these benefits and opportunities is key to crafting successful campaigns and building a thriving online presence. As we delve deeper into strategies and tactics, keep these advantages in mind to maximize the impact of your efforts.

Chapter 2.

Setting Up Your Facebook Business Page

- Step-by-step guide to creating an effective business page

1. Setting Up Your Page:

Start by logging into your personal Facebook account. Navigate to the "Pages" section and click on "Create Page." Choose the "Business or Brand" category, and fill in the required information such as your business name, category, and description.

2. Profile and Cover Photos:

Upload a high-resolution profile picture that represents your brand, such as your logo. Select an eye-catching cover photo that visually communicates your brand identity. Ensure these images are optimized for both desktop and mobile viewing.

3. Complete Your About Section:

Provide essential details about your business in the "About" section. Include a concise yet informative description, contact information, website link, business hours, and any other relevant details. This section serves as a quick overview for visitors.

4. Create a Username and Custom URL:**

Choose a username that is easy to remember and aligns with your brand.

This becomes part of your custom URL (facebook.com/username). A memorable username makes it simpler for users to find and tag your page.

5. Add a Call-to-Action (CTA) Button:
Utilize the CTA button on your page to encourage specific actions, such as "Contact Us," "Shop Now," or "Sign Up." Tailor the button to align with your business objectives and guide visitors toward meaningful interactions.

6. Build Your Page Tabs:
Arrange your page tabs to highlight the most relevant sections. Common tabs include "Home," "About," "Services," "Shop," and more. Customize the order to prioritize the information you want visitors to see first.

7. Content Strategy:

Develop a content strategy that reflects your brand voice and resonates with your target audience. Plan a mix of engaging posts, visuals, and relevant industry content. Consistency is key – aim for a regular posting schedule.

8. Engage Your Audience:

Actively engage with your audience by responding to comments, messages, and reviews promptly. Encourage discussions, ask questions, and create polls to foster a sense of community around your business.

9. Utilize Facebook Insights:

Regularly analyze Facebook Insights to understand your page's performance. Insights provide valuable data on reach, engagement, and audience demographics, helping you refine your content strategy for better results.

10. Run Targeted Ads:

Explore Facebook's advertising options to reach a broader audience. Utilize the ad manager to create targeted campaigns based on demographics, interests, and behaviors. Monitor ad performance and adjust settings as needed.

11. Collaborate and Network:

Leverage Facebook's networking opportunities by collaborating with other businesses, joining relevant groups, and participating in industry discussions. Networking can expand your reach and introduce your brand to new audiences.

12. Regularly Update Information:

Keep your business page current by updating information, adding new products or services, and refreshing visuals. An up-to-date page instills confidence in your audience and showcases your commitment to maintaining a dynamic online presence.

By following these steps, you lay a solid foundation for an effective Facebook business page. Remember, the key to success lies not only in creating the page but in actively managing and optimizing it over time to meet the evolving needs of your business and audience.

- Optimizing page elements for maximum impact

Creating a Facebook business page is just the first step; optimizing its elements is crucial to making a lasting impact on your audience. Here's a guide to help you maximize the effectiveness of your page:

1. Eye-Catching Visuals:

Invest in compelling visuals. Ensure your profile and cover photos are high-quality, on-brand, and instantly convey your business identity. Use images that resonate with your target audience and make a memorable first impression.

2. Concise and Informative About Section:

Craft a concise and informative "About" section. Communicate your business's mission, products, and values. Use language that resonates with your audience and highlights what sets your brand apart.

3. Keyword Optimization:

Optimize your page for search by incorporating relevant keywords in your business description, posts, and other sections. This enhances the discoverability of your page when users search for related topics on Facebook.

4. Custom URL and Username:

Choose a custom URL and username that are easy to remember and reflect your brand. A user-friendly URL makes it simpler for people to find and share your page.

5. Strategic Use of Call-to-Action Button:

Make the most of the call-to-action (CTA) button on your page. Align it with your business goals—whether it's to encourage contact, make a purchase, or sign up for newsletters. The CTA button is a direct gateway to engaging with your business.

6. Highlight Important Tabs:

Arrange your page tabs strategically to emphasize the most important sections. Consider placing essential tabs, like "Shop" or "Services," higher in the tab order for easy access by visitors.

7. Regular and Diverse Content:

Develop a content strategy that includes a mix of posts, images, videos, and other formats. Regularly update your page with diverse content that reflects your brand personality and provides value to your audience.

8. Engagement and Interaction:

Actively engage with your audience by responding to comments, messages, and reviews. Foster a sense of community by asking questions, running polls, and encouraging discussions. An engaged audience is more likely to stay connected and advocate for your brand.

9. Utilize Facebook Insights:

Leverage Facebook Insights to understand your audience's preferences and behaviors. Analyze metrics such as reach, engagement, and page views to refine your content strategy and optimize posting times.

10. Mobile Optimization:

Ensure that your page is optimized for mobile users. With a significant portion of Facebook users accessing the platform on mobile devices, a mobile-friendly page enhances the overall user experience.

11. Consistent Branding:

Maintain consistency in branding across all elements of your page. This includes using the same logo, color scheme, and tone of voice. Consistent branding builds brand recognition and reinforces your business identity.

12. Adapt and Experiment:

Stay adaptable and open to experimenting with different strategies. Monitor the performance of your page elements, be willing to make adjustments, and adapt to the evolving preferences of your audience.

By optimizing these elements, you not only create a visually appealing and engaging Facebook business page but also lay the groundwork for building a strong online presence and connecting with your target audience effectively. Regularly assess and refine these elements to stay ahead in the dynamic world of digital marketing.

Chapter 3.

Understanding Your Audience on Facebook

- Strategies for identifying and targeting your ideal audience

Understanding your audience on Facebook is pivotal to the success of your marketing efforts. By identifying and targeting your ideal audience, you can tailor your content, maximize engagement, and achieve better results. Here are effective strategies to help you in this process:

1. Define Your Buyer Personas:

Start by creating detailed buyer personas – fictional representations of your ideal customers. Consider demographics, interests, behaviors, and challenges. This foundational step helps you align your content with the needs and preferences of your target audience.

2. Utilize Facebook Insights:

Leverage the insights provided by Facebook. Analyze demographic data, page views, and engagement metrics to gain valuable information about your current audience. Identify patterns and trends that can guide your content strategy.

3. Engage in Audience Research:

Conduct thorough audience research to understand the interests and behaviors of your potential customers. Utilize tools like surveys, interviews, and social listening to gather insights directly from your audience.

4. Monitor Competitors:

Keep an eye on your competitors and their interactions with their audience. Analyze the types of content they share, the engagement they receive, and the demographics they target. Extract learnings to enhance your strategy.

5. Utilize Facebook Groups:

Join and participate in relevant Facebook groups related to your industry. Observe discussions, note common challenges, and understand the language used by your audience. This firsthand interaction provides valuable insights.

6. Run Targeted Surveys and Polls:

Use Facebook's built-in tools for running surveys and polls. Ask questions that help you understand your audience's preferences, pain points, and expectations. This direct feedback aids in refining your approach.

7. Analyze Website Analytics:

Integrate Facebook Pixel with your website and analyze the data it provides. Track user behavior, page visits, and conversions. This data helps in creating targeted Facebook ads and content that resonates with your website visitors.

8. Segment Your Audience:

Divide your audience into segments based on demographics, behaviors, or interactions with your content. This segmentation allows for personalized targeting, ensuring that each group receives content tailored to their specific interests.

9. Lookalike Audiences:

Leverage Facebook's Lookalike Audience feature. By identifying common characteristics of your existing audience, Facebook can help you reach new users who share similar traits and are likely interested in your products or services.

10. Stay Responsive to Feedback:

Actively monitor comments, reviews, and messages on your page. Pay attention to the feedback provided by your audience. Use both positive and negative comments as valuable insights to refine your approach.

11. Experiment and Adjust:

Be willing to experiment with different targeting parameters and content types. Monitor the performance of your campaigns and adjust your strategy based on what resonates most with your audience.

12. Regularly Evaluate and Update:

Audience preferences evolve, so it's essential to regularly evaluate and update your understanding of your audience. Stay informed about industry trends, shifts in demographics, and changes in consumer behavior.

By implementing these strategies, you not only identify your ideal audience on Facebook but also create a dynamic understanding that evolves with the changing landscape. This nuanced approach enables you to build meaningful connections and deliver content that truly resonates with those you aim to reach.

- Utilizing Facebook Insights for data-driven decisions

In the dynamic world of Facebook marketing, making informed decisions is crucial for success. Facebook Insights is a powerful tool that provides a wealth of data about your page, audience, and content performance. Here's how you can effectively leverage Facebook Insights to drive data-driven decisions:

1. Understanding Your Audience Demographics:
   Explore the "People" tab in Facebook Insights to gain insights into the demographics of your audience. Understand factors such as age, gender,

location, and language preferences. This information helps tailor your content to better resonate with your audience.

2. Engagement Metrics:

Analyze engagement metrics, including likes, comments, and shares, to gauge the popularity of your content. Identify trends in the type of content that receives the most engagement and adjust your content strategy accordingly.

3. Post Timing and Frequency:

Evaluate the "Posts" tab to determine the timing and frequency of your posts. Identify when your audience is most active and schedule posts accordingly. Adjusting the timing and frequency of your posts can significantly impact reach and engagement.

4. Page Views and Actions:

Monitor the "Page Views" and "Actions on Page" sections to understand how users interact with your page. Track the number of clicks on your contact information, directions, or website links. This information can guide optimizations for a user-friendly experience.

5. Video Performance:

If video content is part of your strategy, delve into the "Videos" tab. Analyze metrics such as views, average watch time, and engagement. Identify patterns in the type and length of videos that capture your audience's attention.

6. Page Reach and Impressions:

Examine the "Reach" and "Impressions" metrics to understand the visibility of your content. Assess the effectiveness of different types of posts in reaching a broader audience. Use this information to refine your content mix.

7. Top Performing Content:

Identify your top-performing content by reviewing the "Top Posts from Pages You Watch" and the "Top Posts" sections. Learn from successful content within your industry and adapt strategies that resonate with your audience.

8. Audience Insights Tool:

Utilize the "Audience Insights" tool to gain deeper insights into your target audience. Understand their interests, behaviors, and preferences beyond Facebook. This information can inform both your content and advertising strategies.

9. Ad Performance:

If you run Facebook ads, assess the performance metrics in the "Ads" tab. Understand the click-through rates, conversion rates, and overall effectiveness of your ads. Use this data to optimize ad targeting and creative elements.

10. Comparative Analysis:

Compare current data with historical data to identify trends and patterns. Look for correlations between specific actions and outcomes, enabling you to refine your strategies based on what has worked well in the past.

11. Set and Track Goals:

Establish specific goals for your Facebook page, such as increasing engagement, driving website traffic, or growing your audience. Regularly track progress against these goals using the metrics provided by Facebook Insights.

12. Iterative Optimization:

Facebook Insights is not a one-time analysis but a continuous tool for improvement. Regularly review and analyze the data, making iterative optimizations to your content, posting schedule, and overall strategy based on the insights gained.

By incorporating Facebook Insights into your decision-making process, you transform your approach from guesswork to strategic precision. The rich data provided empowers you to tailor your content, refine your advertising, and ultimately achieve better results in the dynamic landscape of Facebook marketing.

Chapter 4.

Creating Compelling Content

- Crafting engaging posts, images, and videos

In the competitive realm of social media, the key to capturing attention and building a loyal audience lies in creating compelling content. Whether it's a witty post, an eye-catching image, or a captivating video, here are strategies to craft content that resonates and engages your audience effectively:

Engaging Posts:

1. Know Your Audience:

Understand the preferences, interests, and language of your target audience. Tailor your posts to resonate with their needs and evoke a response.

2. Craft Captivating Headlines:
Capture attention with compelling headlines. Use concise, impactful language that entices users to read further.

3. Use Visuals:
Incorporate images, GIFs, or emojis to complement your text. Visual elements increase engagement and make your posts more shareable.

4. Ask Questions:
Encourage interaction by posing questions. This prompts users to share their opinions and experiences, fostering a sense of community.

5. Share Behind-the-Scenes Content:

Humanize your brand by sharing behind-the-scenes glimpses. This adds authenticity and builds a stronger connection with your audience.

6. Create Contests and Giveaways:

Organize contests or giveaways. This not only boosts engagement but also encourages users to share your content with their network.

7. Utilize Trending Hashtags:

Stay current by incorporating relevant and trending hashtags. This increases the discoverability of your posts among a broader audience.

8. Tell Stories:

Craft narratives that resonate emotionally. Stories have a powerful impact and are more likely to be remembered and shared.

Eye-Catching Images:

1. Maintain Visual Consistency:
   Establish a consistent visual style that aligns with your brand. This consistency fosters brand recognition.

2. Focus on High-Quality:
   Invest in high-quality images. Clear, well-composed visuals not only look more professional but also capture attention more effectively.

3. Utilize Infographics:
   Condense complex information into visually appealing infographics. They are highly shareable and convey information in a digestible format.

4. Include User-Generated Content:
   Showcase content created by your audience. User-generated content adds

authenticity and encourages a sense of community.

5. Create Memes and Humorous Content:
When appropriate for your brand, incorporate humor into your visuals. Memes and humorous content often go viral and increase shareability.

6. Experiment with Carousel Posts:
Utilize carousel posts to share a series of images. This format encourages users to swipe through, increasing engagement and time spent on your content.

Captivating Videos:

1. Optimize for Mobile Viewing:
Given the prevalence of mobile users, ensure your videos are optimized for mobile viewing. Use clear visuals and legible text.

2. Create Short and Snappy Content:

Attention spans are short. Keep your videos concise and impactful to maintain viewer engagement.

3. Tell a Compelling Story:

Craft a narrative in your videos. Whether it's a tutorial, a product showcase, or a customer testimonial, storytelling captivates your audience.

4. Incorporate Captions:

Many users watch videos with the sound off. Include captions to make your content accessible and engaging for all viewers.

5. Leverage Live Video:

Go live to connect with your audience in real time. Live videos often receive higher engagement, and users can interact with you directly.

6. Educational Content:

Share informative and educational content. How-to videos, tutorials, and industry insights establish your brand as an authority in your niche.

7. Add Music or Background Sounds:

Enhance the auditory experience of your videos by adding background music or relevant sounds. This can evoke emotions and make your content more memorable.

Remember, the key to compelling content is understanding your audience, staying authentic to your brand, and continually experimenting with new ideas. By combining these strategies, you can create a diverse and engaging content mix that resonates with your audience on Facebook and beyond.

- Best practices for content that resonates with your audience

Creating content that truly connects with your audience involves a strategic blend of creativity, authenticity, and understanding. Here are best practices to ensure your content resonates effectively:

1. Know Your Audience:

Understand the demographics, preferences, and behaviors of your target audience. Tailor your content to address their needs, interests, and challenges.

2. Define Clear Objectives:

Establish specific goals for your content. Whether it's increasing brand awareness, driving engagement, or promoting a product, clarity on objectives guides your content strategy.

3. Consistent Brand Voice:

Maintain a consistent brand voice across all your content. This builds familiarity and trust among your audience.

4. Quality Over Quantity:

Prioritize quality content over quantity. Well-crafted, valuable content tends to perform better and leave a lasting impression.

5. Tell Compelling Stories:

Craft narratives that resonate emotionally. Stories have a unique ability to captivate and create a memorable impact.

6. Utilize User-Generated Content:

Encourage and showcase content created by your audience. User-generated content adds authenticity and builds a sense of community.

7. Visual Appeal:

Incorporate visually appealing elements into your content. Whether it's eye-catching images, engaging graphics, or well-designed videos, visuals enhance the overall appeal.

8. Diverse Content Mix:

Maintain diversity in your content types. Mix text posts, images, videos, infographics, and more to cater to different preferences within your audience.

9. Personalization:

Personalize your content when possible. Address your audience directly, use their language, and make them feel seen and valued.

10. Engage and Respond:

Actively engage with your audience by responding to comments, messages, and feedback. This fosters a sense of community and strengthens relationships.

11. Utilize Emotion:

Connect with your audience on an emotional level. Content that triggers emotions tends to be more memorable and shareable.

12. Monitor Analytics:

Regularly analyze the performance of your content through analytics. Understand what works well and use these insights to refine your future content strategy.

13. Consistent Posting Schedule:

Establish a consistent posting schedule. Regular, predictable content keeps your audience engaged and aware of when to expect updates.

14. A/B Testing:

Experiment with A/B testing to understand what resonates best with your audience. Test different headlines, visuals, or posting times to optimize your approach.

15. Educate and Add Value:

Provide educational content that adds value to your audience. How-to guides, tutorials, and insightful industry information position your brand as a valuable resource.

16. Stay Authentic:

Be authentic in your communication. Authenticity builds trust, and transparent communication resonates more profoundly with audiences.

17. Monitor Trends:

Stay informed about industry trends and popular topics. Incorporating relevant trends into your content keeps it fresh and aligned with current interests.

18. Encourage User Interaction:

Prompt user interaction through polls, quizzes, and questions. Engaging content invites participation and strengthens the bond between your brand and audience.

19. Optimize for Mobile:

Given the prevalence of mobile users, ensure that your content is optimized for mobile viewing. This guarantees accessibility across a wide range of devices.

20. Evaluate and Iterate:

Continuously evaluate the performance of your content and be willing to iterate. The digital landscape evolves, and adapting your strategy ensures ongoing relevance.

By adhering to these best practices, you create a content strategy that not only captures attention but also builds lasting connections with your audience. Regularly reassess and refine your approach based on audience feedback and changing trends to maintain a dynamic and effective content strategy.

Chapter 5.

Effective Advertising on Facebook

- Introduction to Facebook Ads Manager

In the ever-expanding digital landscape, leveraging the power of Facebook Ads is essential for businesses aiming to reach and engage their target audience effectively. Facebook Ads Manager serves as the central hub for creating, managing, and optimizing advertising campaigns on the platform. Here's an introduction to help you navigate this powerful tool:

Understanding Facebook Ads Manager:

1. Accessing Ads Manager:

Facebook Ads Manager is accessible through your Facebook account. Simply navigate to the dropdown menu on the top right corner, click on "Ad Center," and choose "Ads Manager."

2. Dashboard Overview:

The Ads Manager dashboard provides an at-a-glance view of your advertising campaigns. Here, you can monitor performance metrics, view active campaigns, and access various tools for campaign creation and analysis.

3. Campaign Structure:

Facebook Ads Manager follows a hierarchical structure: Campaigns, Ad Sets, and Ads. A campaign represents your overarching objective, ad sets define your target audience and budget, and individual ads showcase your creative content.

4. Objective Selection:

When creating a campaign, choose a specific objective aligned with your marketing goals. Whether it's driving traffic, generating leads, or increasing brand awareness, selecting the right objective is crucial.

Creating Effective Ads:

1. Audience Targeting:

Leverage detailed audience targeting options. Define your audience based on demographics, interests, behaviors, and even custom audiences. This precision ensures your ads reach the most relevant users.

2. Ad Placement:

Facebook offers various ad placements, including the Facebook News Feed, Instagram, Audience Network, and more.

Tailor your ad placements based on where your audience is most active.

3. Budget and Schedule:

Set a clear budget for your campaign and allocate it across ad sets. Define your schedule to control when your ads are displayed. The budget optimization feature ensures optimal spending for the best results.

4. Compelling Ad Creatives:

Craft visually appealing and engaging ad creatives. Use high-quality images or videos, attention-grabbing headlines, and concise ad copy. A/B testing can help identify the most effective creative elements.

5. Ad Formats:

Experiment with different ad formats, such as carousel ads, slideshow ads, or dynamic ads. Choosing the right format enhances the visual appeal and impact of your advertising.

Monitoring and Optimization:

1. Performance Metrics:
Regularly monitor performance metrics within Ads Manager. Key metrics include reach, engagement, clicks, and conversions. Analyzing these metrics guides optimization efforts.

2. Split Testing:
Implement split testing to compare different elements of your ads. Test variations in audience targeting, ad creatives, and placements to identify the most effective combinations.

3. Pixel Integration:
Integrate the Facebook Pixel with your website. This powerful tool tracks user interactions and provides valuable data

for optimizing ad delivery and measuring conversions.

4. Ad Schedule Adjustments:

Review the performance of your ads over time and adjust the ad schedule if needed. Focusing on peak times of user activity can maximize your ad's visibility.

5. Budget Reallocation:

Based on performance insights, reallocate your budget to high-performing ad sets or tweak audience targeting for better results. This ongoing optimization ensures efficient spending.

Ad Reporting:

1. Custom Reports:

Utilize the reporting features in Ads Manager to create custom reports. Tailor the data you view to align with your specific key performance indicators (KPIs) and goals.

2. Attribution Modeling:

Understand the customer journey by exploring attribution models. This feature helps attribute conversions to different touchpoints in the user's interaction with your ads.

3. Exporting Data:

Export campaign data for in-depth analysis. This allows for comprehensive evaluation beyond the Ads Manager interface and facilitates collaboration with team members.

However, mastering Facebook Ads Manager empowers advertisers to create, optimize, and analyze campaigns with precision. This introduction lays the groundwork for navigating the tool effectively, but continuous exploration and adaptation are key to staying ahead in the dynamic landscape of digital advertising.

- Designing and optimizing ad campaigns for success

In the ever-evolving landscape of digital marketing, designing and optimizing ad campaigns on platforms like Facebook is pivotal for achieving success and reaching your target audience effectively. Here's a comprehensive guide to help you create and refine ad campaigns that deliver optimal results:

1. Clear Campaign Objectives:

Define Your Goals: Clearly articulate the objectives of your campaign. Whether it's driving traffic, generating leads, or increasing brand awareness, a well-defined goal sets the foundation for a successful campaign.

2. Audience Targeting Precision:

Know Your Audience: Utilize detailed audience targeting options. Define your audience based on demographics, interests, behaviors, and even custom audiences. Precise targeting ensures your ads reach the most relevant users.

3. Compelling Ad Creatives:

Visual Appeal: Craft visually appealing and engaging ad creatives. Use high-quality images or videos, attention-grabbing headlines, and concise ad copy. A compelling creative is key to capturing the audience's attention.

4. A/B Testing:

Experiment and Optimize: Implement A/B testing to compare different elements of your ads. Test variations in audience targeting, ad creatives, and placements to identify the most effective combinations. Optimize based on results.

5. Diverse Ad Formats:

Explore Options: Experiment with different ad formats, such as carousel ads, slideshow ads, or video ads. Choosing the right format enhances the visual appeal and impact of your advertising.

6. Strategic Ad Placement:

Select Relevant Placements: Consider where your audience is most active. Facebook offers various ad placements, including the News Feed, Instagram, Audience Network, and more. Tailor your ad placements accordingly.

7. Set a Clear Budget:

Allocate Budget Wisely: Define a clear budget for your campaign and allocate it across ad sets. Use budget optimization to ensure optimal spending for the best results. Regularly monitor and adjust as needed.

8. Ad Schedule Optimization:

Timing Matters: Analyze when your audience is most active and adjust your ad schedule accordingly. Focusing on peak times enhances the visibility and performance of your ads.

9. Harness the Power of Retargeting:

Utilize Retargeting Strategies: Implement retargeting using tools like the Facebook Pixel. This allows you to re-engage users who have interacted with your website, maximizing conversion opportunities.

10. Monitor Key Metrics:

Data-Driven Decisions: Regularly monitor key performance metrics within your ad manager. Metrics like reach, engagement, clicks, and conversions provide valuable insights for data-driven decision-making.

11. Responsive Ad Design:

Mobile Optimization:** With the prevalence of mobile users, ensure that your ads are optimized for mobile viewing. A responsive design guarantees accessibility across various devices.

12. Ad Copy Effectiveness:

Craft Persuasive Copy: Write compelling ad copy that communicates your message. Focus on value propositions and calls to action to encourage user engagement.

13. Landing Page Alignment:

Seamless Transition: Ensure alignment between your ad content and the landing page. A seamless transition provides a positive user experience and improves conversion rates.

14. Regular Review and Optimization:

Iterate Based on Data: Continuously review the performance of your ads and be willing to iterate. Adjust targeting parameters, creative elements, and budgets based on the insights gained.

15. Comprehensive Reporting:

Custom Reports and Analytics: Utilize reporting features to create custom reports aligned with your key performance indicators (KPIs). Export campaign data for in-depth analysis and collaboration.

16. Stay Adaptable:

Adapt to Changes: The digital landscape is dynamic. Stay adaptable to changes in audience behavior, platform algorithms, and industry trends. Adaptation ensures ongoing relevance and effectiveness.

By following these strategies, you establish a solid foundation for designing and optimizing ad campaigns that resonate with your audience and drive meaningful results. Remember, successful campaigns are not static – continuous evaluation and refinement are essential for staying ahead in the competitive world of digital advertising.

Chapter 6.

Measuring and Analyzing Results

- Overview of key metrics and analytics tools

Effectively measuring and analyzing the results of your ad campaigns is crucial for making informed decisions and optimizing future strategies. Here's an overview of key metrics and analytics tools to help you gauge the success of your efforts:

1. Key Metrics for Ad Campaigns:

a. Impressions:

- Definition: The number of times your ad is displayed.
- Importance: Indicates the reach and visibility of your campaign.

b. Click-Through Rate (CTR):
- Definition: The percentage of people who clicked on your ad after seeing it.
- Importance: Reflects the ad's relevance and engagement level.

c. Conversion Rate:
- Definition: The percentage of users who completed the desired action (e.g., made a purchase) after clicking on the ad.
- Importance: Measures the effectiveness of your campaign in driving conversions.

d. Cost Per Click (CPC):
- Definition: The average cost you pay for each click on your ad.

- Importance: Helps evaluate the cost-effectiveness of your campaign.

e. Return on Ad Spend (ROAS):
   - Definition: The revenue generated for every dollar spent on advertising.
   - Importance: Indicates the profitability and overall performance of your campaign.

f. Engagement Metrics:
   - Definition: Likes, comments, shares, and other interactions with your ad.
   - *Importance:* Measures the level of audience engagement and interaction.

g. Ad Frequency:
   - Definition: The average number of times a user sees your ad.
   - Importance: Helps prevent ad fatigue and ensures varied exposure.

2. Facebook Ads Manager Insights:

a. Ad Performance:
- Insight: Analyze ad performance metrics such as reach, engagement, and clicks within the Ads Manager dashboard.

b. Audience Insights:
- Insight: Utilize the Audience Insights tool to gain a deeper understanding of your target audience's demographics, interests, and behaviors.

c. Conversion Tracking:
- *Insight:* Integrate the Facebook Pixel with your website to track user actions, measure conversions, and optimize for specific events.

d. Ad Reports:
- Insight: Create custom ad reports to visualize and analyze data aligned with your campaign objectives and KPIs.

3. Google Analytics:

a. Website Traffic:
- Insight: Track the traffic driven to your website from Facebook ads. Analyze user behavior and navigation patterns.

b. Goal Conversions:
- Insight: Set up goals in Google Analytics to measure specific actions on your website, such as form submissions or product purchases.

c. User Flow:
- Insight: Visualize the path users take on your website after clicking on a Facebook ad. Identify drop-off points and areas for improvement.

4. Hotjar:

a. Heatmaps:

- Insight: Use heatmaps to understand where users are clicking and interacting on your website. Identify areas of interest and potential friction points.

b. Session Recordings:
   - Insight: Watch recordings of user sessions to gain qualitative insights into user behavior, preferences, and potential issues.

5. Third-Party Analytics Platforms:

a. Social Media Analytics Tools:
   - Insight: Platforms like Hootsuite, Buffer, or Sprout Social offer in-depth social media analytics, providing additional perspectives on campaign performance.

b. Conversion Platforms:
   - Insight: For e-commerce, platforms like Shopify or WooCommerce provide

insights into product sales and conversion data.

6. Continuous Optimization:

a. Regular Review and Adjustment:
- Practice: Regularly review the performance metrics of your campaigns. Adjust targeting, creative elements, and budgets based on insights gained.

b. Adaptation to Trends:
- Practice: Stay adaptable to changes in audience behavior, platform algorithms, and industry trends. Adaptation ensures ongoing relevance and effectiveness.

Measuring and analyzing these key metrics, along with utilizing analytics tools, provides a holistic view of your ad campaign's performance. Continuous optimization based on insights gained is the key to achieving sustained success in the dynamic world of digital advertising.

- Interpreting data to refine and improve your Facebook marketing strategy

Interpreting data is a critical aspect of refining and enhancing your Facebook marketing strategy. The insights derived from analytics enable you to make informed decisions, optimize campaigns, and ultimately achieve better results. Here's a comprehensive guide on how to interpret data effectively for continuous improvement:

1. Analyzing Key Performance Metrics:

a. Impressions and Reach:

- *Interpretation:* Evaluate the visibility of your content. A high number of impressions and reach indicates effective exposure to your target audience.

b. Click-Through Rate (CTR):

- Interpretation: A high CTR suggests that your ad is resonating with the audience. Conversely, a low CTR may indicate the need for adjustments in targeting or creative elements.

c. Conversion Rate:

- Interpretation: A higher conversion rate signifies that your audience is taking the desired action. Analyze which campaigns or ad sets drive the most conversions and refine accordingly.

d. Cost Per Click (CPC) and Return on Ad Spend (ROAS):
   - Interpretation: Assess the efficiency of your spending. A lower CPC and a higher ROAS indicate cost-effective campaigns. Adjust budgets and targeting based on these insights.

2. Audience Insights:

a. Demographics and Interests:
   - Interpretation: Understand the characteristics of your audience. Identify demographics and interests that respond positively to your content, and tailor future campaigns accordingly.

b. Geographic Data:
   - Interpretation: Analyze the geographic locations where your ads perform well. Optimize targeting for regions with higher engagement and

adjust content to resonate with local preferences.

3. Ad Placement and Format:

a. Placement Performance:

- Interpretation: Evaluate the performance across different ad placements. Determine whether your audience engages more on Facebook, Instagram, or other networks. Adjust budgets based on platform effectiveness.

b. Ad Format Effectiveness:

- Interpretation: Assess the impact of different ad formats. Identify whether carousel ads, videos, or image-based ads resonate best with your audience. Allocate resources to the most effective formats.

4. Behavior Analysis:

a. User Interaction:

- Interpretation: Examine user interactions with your ads. Identify patterns in comments, likes, and shares. Engage with your audience based on their responses to foster community and loyalty.

b. Device and Platform Usage:

- Interpretation: Understand the devices and platforms your audience predominantly uses. Optimize content for mobile if most interactions occur on smartphones.

5. Conversion Tracking and Attribution Models:

a. Conversion Path Analysis:

- Interpretation: Analyze the user journey leading to conversions. Understand the touchpoints and refine your strategy to enhance the effectiveness of each stage in the conversion funnel.

b. Attribution Models:
- Interpretation: Evaluate the attribution model that best reflects your audience's behavior. Whether it's first-click, last-click, or multi-touch attribution, choose the model that aligns with your campaign goals.

6. Heatmaps and User Recordings:

a. Interaction Patterns:
- Interpretation: Use heatmaps to visualize where users interact most on your website. Analyze user recordings to identify navigation patterns and potential pain points.

7. Feedback and Sentiment Analysis:

a. Comments and Reviews:

- Interpretation: Pay attention to user comments and reviews. Positive sentiments indicate successful engagement, while negative sentiments may reveal areas for improvement.

8. Regular Review and Iteration:

a. Continuous Optimization:
    - Interpretation: Regularly review campaign performance and be willing to iterate. Adapt based on changing audience behaviors, trends, and insights gained from data analysis.

b. Experimentation and A/B Testing:
    - Interpretation: Conduct experiments and A/B testing to validate assumptions. Identify the most effective variations and implement them into your ongoing strategy.

9. Adapting to Trends and Industry Changes:

a. Industry Landscape:
   - Interpretation: Stay informed about industry trends and changes. Adapt your strategy to align with evolving consumer behaviors and emerging technologies.

10. Collaborative Analysis:

a. Cross-Team Collaboration:
   - Interpretation: Foster collaboration between marketing, analytics, and creative teams. Shared insights and collaborative analysis lead to a comprehensive understanding of campaign performance.

Interpreting data is an ongoing process that requires a keen eye for patterns, a commitment to continuous improvement, and a willingness to adapt.

By systematically analyzing key metrics, audience insights, and user behaviors, you can refine your Facebook marketing strategy to be more targeted, engaging, and ultimately successful in achieving your business objectives.

www.ingramcontent.com/pod-product-compliance
Lightning Source LLC
LaVergne TN
LVHW051537050326
832903LV00033B/4303